A+
books

Words I Know

A Backpack Full of Verbs

by Bette Blaisdell

Content Consultant:
Terry Flaherty, PhD
Professor of English
Minnesota State University, Mankato

CAPSTONE PRESS
a capstone imprint

A+ Books are published by Capstone Press,
1710 Roe Crest Drive, North Mankato, Minnesota 56003
www.capstonepub.com

Library of Congress Cataloging-in-Publication Data
Cataloging-in-publication information is on file with the Library of Congress.
ISBN 978-1-4765-3936-2 (library binding)
ISBN 978-1-4765-5096-1 (paperback)
ISBN 978-1-4765-5941-4 (ebook PDF)

Editorial Credits
Jill Kalz, editor; Juliette Peters, designer; Svetlana Zhurkin, media researcher;
Kathy McColley, production specialist

Photo Credits
Shutterstock: 2xSamara, 5 (left), AKaiser, 2–3, 4–5 (back), 32, Alex Staroseltsev, 4 (top), Alexander Takiev, 15
(bottom), Anan Kaewkhammul, 14 (bottom), Andrew Burgess, cover (frog), artcphotos, 28 (bottom), Aspen
Photo, 10 (right), BlueOrange Studio, 22 (bottom), Brandon Alms, 25 (top), creative, 28 (top), Dennis Donohue,
15 (top), design56, cover (backpack), Digital Genetics, 10 (left), Digital Media Pro, 21 (top), Eva Gruendemann,
9 (bottom), Gelpi JM, 13, gorillaimages, 6 (right), jordache, 23, Kafer photo, 7 (bottom), konmesa, 25 (bottom),
L_amica, 19 (top), lightpoet, 9 (top), LittleMiss, 5 (top), Mandy Godbehear, 16 (bottom), 21 (bottom), Maram, 11
(top), Mihai Blanaru, 7 (top), Monkey Business Images, 4 (bottom), 17, 18 (right), mrkornflakes, 8, NatalieJean,
11 (bottom), Nelosa, 19 (bottom), njaj, 14 (top), Nuiiko, 20 (top), Odua Images, 18 (left), Peter Schwarz, 24, red-
feniks, 30–31, Rick Becker-Leckrone, 27 (bottom), Ryszard Stelmachowicz, 22 (top), Samuel Borges Photography,
6 (left), spotmatik, 26 (top), Stefan Petru Andronache, 1, Stephanie Frey, 16 (top), Stuart Monk, 12, Studio 1One,
20 (bottom), Suzanne Tucker, 27 (top), tammykayphoto, 26 (bottom), wavebreakmedia, 19 (middle), Wollertz, 29

Note to Parents, Teachers, and Librarians
This Words I Know book uses full color photographs and a nonfiction format to introduce the concept of
language and parts of speech. *A Backpack Full of Verbs* is designed to be read aloud to a pre-reader or to be
read independently by an early reader. Photographs help listeners and early readers understand the text
and concepts discussed. The book encourages further learning by including the following sections: Table of
Contents, Read More, and Internet Sites. Early readers may need assistance using these features.

Printed in the United States of America in Stevens Point, Wisconsin.
092013   007773WZS14

Table of Contents

What's a Verb?

What would happen
if we didn't have verbs?

Nothing.

A rabbit couldn't *jump*.
A clock couldn't *tick*.
You couldn't *laugh* or *cheer*.

A **verb** is one part of speech. It shows what people or things do or what they are.

Jump, *tick*, *laugh*, and *cheer* are words that show what something does. They're called action verbs.

Being verbs connect, or link, the subject of a sentence with facts about it. Marco *is* on the team. I *am* funny. Being verbs are also called linking verbs.

What verbs do you carry in *your* backpack?

On the Dance Floor

Have you learned a brand-new dance?
Or are there ants inside your pants?

shimmy
sway
boogie
twirl

shuffle
spin
twist

whirl

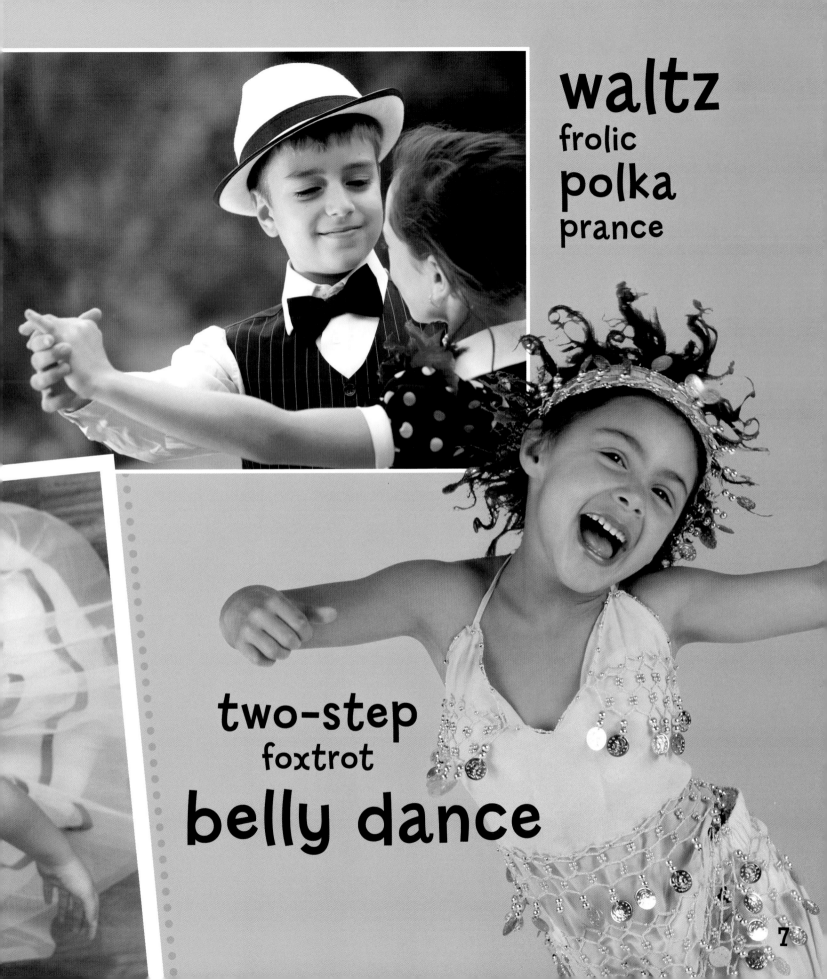

waltz
frolic
polka
prance

two-step
foxtrot
belly dance

7

What's Cooking?

Cooking in the kitchen, so much to do!
I'm getting hungry. How about you?

pinch **measure** peel

slice

stir
cut
chop
dice

8

boil
fry
poach
rinse

sautee
bake
steam

mince

This, Not That

Opposites are as different as can be.
How many opposites do you see?

win/lose
stop/go

walk/run
catch/throw

add/subtract
float/sink

push/pull

stare/
blink

Take a Look

See that mirror on the wall?
Your face can smile, but that's not all!

frown
grin
grimace
blush

beam
scowl
sulk
flush

smirk sneer giggle quiver

pucker pout laugh shiver

13

Animal Talk

Did you hear a crazy sound?
Was that a moose? A mouse? A hound?

oink

bark

buzz

moo

squeak

hiss

whistle

coo

quack
squeal
trumpet
growl

gurgle
chirp
roar
howl

Move It

You could just walk, but here's a dare:
How else can you get from here to there?

slink

sneak

shuffle

clomp

sprint

gallop

hop

stomp

skip

lumber

mosey

stride

tip-toe

limp

stroll

glide

Class Time

The bell says it's time to start.
Do you love school with all your heart?

answer

spell

ask

recite

read

print

draw

write

listen
group
divide
erase

multiply

9 x 5 = 45

and
punctuate

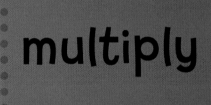

Recess

Everyone needs a little break.
Get out, get loose, wriggle, and shake!

climb
bounce
bat
slide

tumble
tag
share
hide

kick

dunk

topple

vault

toss

race

somersault

Today's Weather

Will the sun shine? Will a rainbow glow?
Peek out your door, and you will know!

rain
hail
sprinkle
drizzle

mist
rumble
thunder
mizzle

freeze

gust

swelter

snow

flood

sleet

bluster

blow

Into the Wild

How animals move is cool, it's true.
They slither and creep and fly. Can you?

scamper

squirm

wallow

pounce

lunge

trot

swoop

bounce

stampede
flutter
dive
wiggle

crawl
scurry
stalk
jiggle

Batter Up

Grab your gear, and pick your teams.
Sports make any day better, it seems.

pitch
skate
cheer
bike

volley
dribble
steal
spike

sweat
swing
lob
bunt

serve
score
snap
punt

Taking Flight

Of course they fly. That we know.
But can birds laugh or do-si-do?

peck
preen
squawk
roost

crow
flock
strut
hoot

migrate
nest
honk
twitter

wade
warble
screech
flitter

Like a Diamond

Late at night the stars say, "Hi!"
When morning comes they say, "Good-bye!"

twinkle
sparkle
glisten
shimmer

glow
flicker
wink
glimmer

flash

blaze

radiate

glint

gleam

illuminate

Read More

Fandel, Jennifer. *What Is a Verb?* Parts of Speech. North Mankato, Minn.: Capstone Press, 2013.

Ganeri, Anita. *Action Words: Verbs.* Getting to Grips with Grammar. Chicago: Heinemann Library, 2012.

Riggs, Kate. *Verbs.* Grammar Basics. Mankato, Minn.: Creative Education, 2013.

Internet Sites

FactHound offers a safe, fun way to find Internet sites related to this book. All of the sites on FactHound have been researched by our staff.

Here's all you do:

Visit *www.facthound.com*

Type in this code: 9781476539362

Super-cool stuff! Check out projects, games and lots more at **www.capstonekids.com**